Mrs Wordsmith®

YEAR 1 ENGLISH

GARGANTUAN WORKBOOK

mrswordsmith.com

Bearnice

Bogart

Brick

Grit

Yin & Yang

Plato

Armie

Shang High

Oz

MEET THE
CHARACTERS

CONTENTS

PHONICS & PHONOLOGICAL AWARENESS

can you say?

ai

paint

AI	**ai**
upper case	lower case

Vowel sounds can be long or short. Long vowels can be made with a single letter or a digraph (two letters making one sound).

The sound of **a** in **apple** is a short vowel sound. The sound of **ai** in **paint** is a long vowel sound.

FIND IT

Can you find the letters for the **ai** sound that are in the words in bold? Circle them.

Plato **painted** a **portrait** with his **tail**.

1. Read each sound.
   Read each sound again
   faster. Read the sounds
   together smoothly.

2. Trace the dotted letter.
   Follow Bogart's emoji.

3. Trace and write the letters.

POWER UPS

Blend the letters
to read the words.

sail   tail   rain

can you say?

ee

seek

EE
upper case

ee
lower case

Can you find the letters for the **ee** sound that are in the words in bold? Circle them.

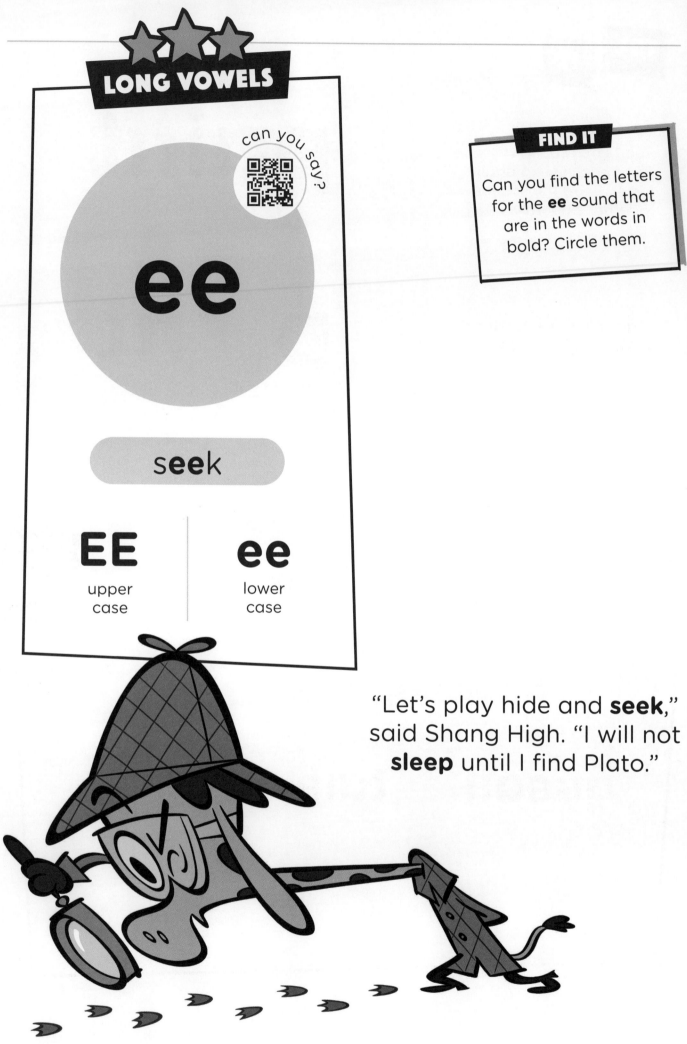

"Let's play hide and **seek**," said Shang High. "I will not **sleep** until I find Plato."

1. Read each sound. Read each sound again faster. Read the sounds together smoothly.

2. Trace the dotted letter. Follow Bogart's emoji.

3. Trace and write the letters.

POWER UPS

Blend the letters to read the words.

queen   bee   sheep

can you say?

igh

fight

IGH
upper case

igh goes in the middle or at the end of the word

Can you find the letters for the **igh** sound that are in the words in bold? Circle them.

"I will **fight** for the treasure with all my **might**!"

1. Read each sound. Read each sound again faster. Read the sounds together smoothly.

2. Trace the dotted letter. Follow Bogart's emoji.

3. Trace and write the letters.

POWER UPS

Blend the letters to read the words.

right   **night**   **high**

oa

can you say?

soak

OA
upper
case

oa
lower
case

Can you find the letters for the **oa** sound that are in the words in bold? Circle them.

Bearnice **soaked** her hair in **soapy** water.

1. Read each sound.
   Read each sound again
   faster. Read the sounds
   together smoothly.

2. Trace the dotted letter.
   Follow Bogart's emoji.

3. Trace and write the letters.

POWER UPS

Blend the letters
to read the words.

boat   **road**   **soap**

can you say?

oo

shampoo

oo
upper case

oo goes in the middle or at the end of the word

FIND IT

Can you find the letters for the **oo** sound that are in the words in bold? Circle them.

"Oops!"

Bearnice put **too** much **shampoo** on her hair!

16

1. Read each sound.
   Read each sound again
   faster. Read the sounds
   together smoothly.

shampoo

2. Trace the dotted letter.
   Follow Bogart's emoji.

shampoo

3. Trace and write the letters.

POWER UPS

Blend the letters
to read the words.

too   food   room

VOWEL SOUNDS

SHORT VOWELS

a
cat

e
bed

i
fish

o
sock

u
sun

LONG VOWELS

ai
rain

ee
feet

igh
night

oa
boat

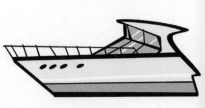

oo
boot

FIND THE VOWEL

Is the vowel long or short?
Write **S** in the box if the vowel is short.
Write **L** in the box if the vowel is long.

rain ☐ l

cat ☐

paint ☐

egg ☐

feet ☐

bed ☐

night ☐

pig ☐

milk ☐

mop ☐

goat ☐

boat ☐

duck ☐

boot ☐

sun ☐

19

SHORT OR LONG VOWEL A

Vowel sounds can be long or short. Long vowels can be made with a single letter or a digraph (two letters making one sound).

The sound of **a** in **apple** is a short vowel sound. The sound of **ai** in **rain** is a long vowel sound.

First, choose the correct word to match to the image.
Next, circle **S** if the vowel is **short** or circle **L** if the vowel is **long**.

---

cat | paint | ant | rain

1.

paint

S | (L)

2.

S | L

3.

S | L

4.

S | L

SHORT OR LONG VOWEL E

The sound of **e** in **bed** is a short vowel sound.
The sound of **ee** in **green** is a long vowel sound.

red | feet | sheep | nest

1.

sheep

S | (L)

2.

S | L

3.

S | L

4.

S | L

Vowel sounds can be long or short. Long vowels can be made with a single letter or a digraph (two letters making one sound).

The sound of **i** in **big** is a short vowel sound. The sound of **igh** in **fight** is a long vowel sound.

First, choose the correct word to match to the image.
Next, circle **S** if the vowel is **short** or circle **L** if the vowel is **long**.

| light | ring | night | fish |

1.

fish

S | L

2.

S | L

3.

S | L

4.

S | L

SHORT OR LONG VOWEL O

The sound of **o** in **mop** is a short vowel sound.
The sound of **oa** in **soap** is a long vowel sound.

---

toast | toad | box | dog

1.

toad

S | **L**

2.

S | L

3.

S | L

4.

S | L

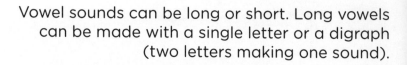 **SHORT OR LONG VOWEL U**

Vowel sounds can be long or short. Long vowels can be made with a single letter or a digraph (two letters making one sound).

The sound of **u** in **tub** is a short vowel sound.
The sound of **oo** in **boot** is a long vowel sound.

First, choose the correct word to match to the image.
Next, circle **S** if the vowel is **short** or circle **L** if the vowel is **long**.

| sun | shampoo | food | bug |

1.

sun

Ⓢ | L

2.

- - - - - - - - - - - - - - -

S | L

3.

- - - - - - - - - - - - - - -

S | L

4.

- - - - - - - - - - - - - - -

S | L

Sort out the short and long vowel words. Write the short vowel words on the left and long vowel words on the right.

SORT THE WORDS

bag soap room milk frog

high ant sail sun bee

SHORT VOWEL WORDS

bag

LONG VOWEL WORDS

can you say?

oo

b**oo**k

OO
upper
case

Remember! The same grapheme (letter or letters) can represent more than one sound.

FIND IT

Can you find the letters for the **oo** sound that are in the words in bold? Circle them.

Armie **took** his time. He **looked** carefully at every picture in the **book**.

1. Read each sound. Read each sound again faster. Read the sounds together smoothly.

2. Trace the dotted letter. Follow Bogart's emoji.

3. Trace and write the letters.

POWER UPS

Blend the letters to read the words.

look   **good**   **took**

can you say?

ar

alarm

AR
upper case

ar
lower case

Can you find the letters for the **ar** sound that are in the words in bold? Circle them.

Grit couldn't move his **arm** to turn off the **large alarm**.

1. Read each sound. Read each sound again faster. Read the sounds together smoothly.

2. Trace the dotted letter. Follow Bogart's emoji.

3. Trace and write the letters.

POWER UPS

Blend the letters to read the words.

car   **part**   **bark**

can you say?

or

sp**or**t

OR
upper
case

or
lower
case

Can you find the letters for the **or** sound that are in the words in bold? Circle them.

Oz was good at every **sport**.

1. Read each sound.
   Read each sound again
   faster. Read the sounds
   together smoothly.

2. Trace the dotted letter.
   Follow Bogart's emoji.

3. Trace and write the letters.

POWER UPS

Blend the letters
to read the words.

born   **fork**   **cord**

can you say?

ur

surf

UR	**ur**
upper case	lower case

Can you find the letters for the **ur** sound that are in the words in bold? Circle them.

Brick loved to **surf** with the **turtles** and the fish.

1. Read each sound.
   Read each sound again
   faster. Read the sounds
   together smoothly.

surf

2. Trace the dotted letter.
   Follow Bogart's emoji.

3. Trace and write the letters.

POWER UPS

Blend the letters
to read the words.

burn   **curl**   **fur**

can you say?

OW

howl

OW	ow
upper case	lower case

Plato always **howls** when the **shower** is full **power**.

34

1. Read each sound.
   Read each sound again
   faster. Read the sounds
   together smoothly.

2. Trace the dotted letter.
   Follow Bogart's emoji.

3. Trace and write the letters.

POWER UPS

Blend the letters
to read the words.

cow   down   now

SORT THE SHORT & LONG VOWEL WORDS

Sort out the short and long vowel words. Write the short vowel words on the left and long vowel words on the right.

SORT THE WORDS

map hat feet coin night

man plum tree duck join

SHORT VOWEL WORDS

map

LONG VOWEL WORDS

SORT THE WORDS

hot mop point moon stuck
tooth queen tail cap kit

SHORT VOWEL WORDS

hot

LONG VOWEL WORDS

can you say?

oi

coin

Oi	oi
upper case	lower case

FIND IT

Can you find the letters for the **oi** sound that are in the words in bold? Circle them.

Armie **pointed** at the **coins** and said, "Let's count them."

1. Read each sound. Read each sound again faster. Read the sounds together smoothly.

2. Trace the dotted letter. Follow Bogart's emoji.

3. Trace and write the letters.

POWER UPS

Blend the letters to read the words.

join   point

39

can you say?

ear

fear

EAR
upper case

ear
lower case

Can you find the letters for the **ear** sound that are in the words in bold? Circle them.

She jumped with **fear** when a spider **appeared**.

1. Read each sound.
   Read each sound again
   faster. Read the sounds
   together smoothly.

2. Trace the dotted letter.
   Follow Bogart's emoji.

3. Trace and write the letters.

POWER UPS

Blend the letters
to read the words.

ear   **hear**   **year**

can you say?

air

hair

AIR
upper
case

air
lower
case

FIND IT

Can you find the letters for the **air** sound that are in the words in bold? Circle them.

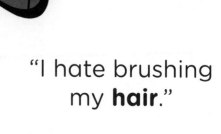

"It's not **fair**!" grumbled Grit.

"I hate brushing my **hair**."

TRY IT

1. Read each sound.
   Read each sound again
   faster. Read the sounds
   together smoothly.

2. Trace the dotted letter.
   Follow Bogart's emoji.

3. Trace and write the letters.

POWER UPS

Blend the letters
to read the words.

pair   chair   fair

LONG VOWELS

can you say?

ure

cure

URE

upper case

ure goes in the middle or at the end of the word

FIND IT

Can you find the letters for the **ure** sound that are in the words in bold? Circle them.

"I've found the **cure**!" cried Armie.

44

1. Read each sound.
   Read each sound again
   faster. Read the sounds
   together smoothly.

cure

2. Trace the dotted letter.
   Follow Bogart's emoji.

3. Trace and write the letters.

POWER UPS

Blend the letters
to read the words.

sure   **pure**   **lure**

can you say?

er

mermaid

ER	er
upper case	lower case

"A **mermaid** is part **person**, part fish," explained Plato.

1. Read each sound.
   Read each sound again
   faster. Read the sounds
   together smoothly.

mermaid

2. Trace the dotted letter.
   Follow Bogart's emoji.

3. Trace and write the letters.

POWER UPS

Blend the letters
to read the words.

her   boxer   herb

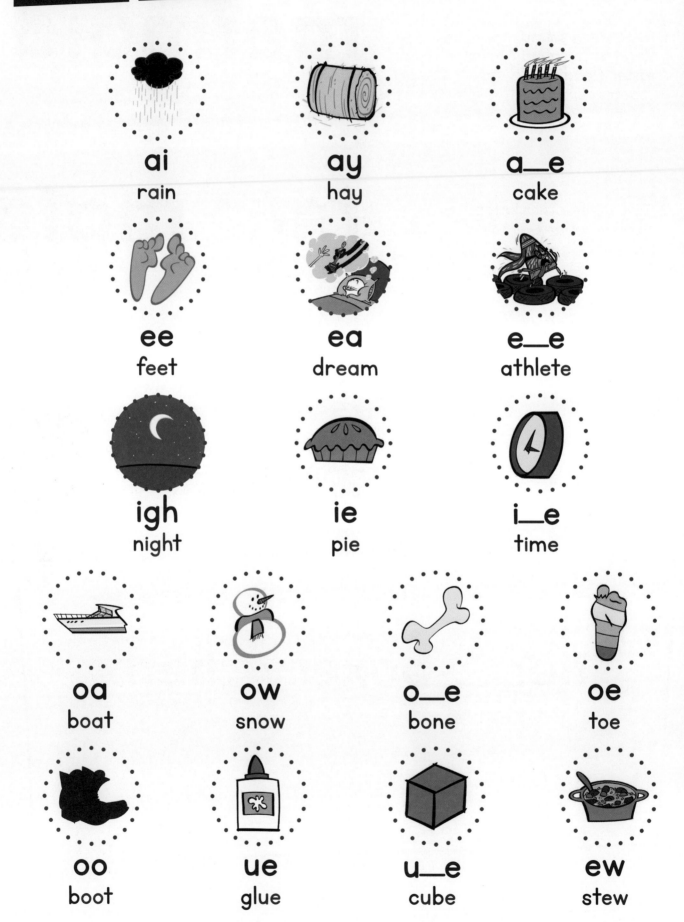

ai
rain

ay
hay

a_e
cake

ee
feet

ea
dream

e_e
athlete

igh
night

ie
pie

i_e
time

oa
boat

ow
snow

o_e
bone

oe
toe

oo
boot

ue
glue

u_e
cube

ew
stew

LONG VOWELS: ADDING e

Write out these words, add **e**, and see how the pronounciation and meaning changes.

Draw a curved line to show the two letters making the long vowel sound.

1.

cap   cape

2.

can

49

LONG VOWELS: ADDING e

Adding e can turn a short vowel into a long vowel.

3.

kit _____

_____

4.

rob _____

_____

Write out these words, add **e**, and see how the pronounciation and meaning changes.

Draw a curved line to show the two letters making the long vowel sound.

5.	**cub**	-----------------------------------
6.	**tap**	-----------------------------------
7.	**cut**	-----------------------------------
8.	**hat**	-----------------------------------

Two vowels can work together as a vowel team. This is called a digraph, when two letters make a single sound.

Underline the vowel digraph and then circle the picture that matches the word.

1. t<u>oa</u>d

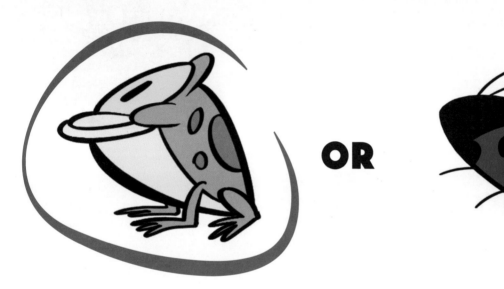

OR

2. **beach**

OR

The first vowel in the team is bold.
It says its name, making a long vowel sound.
The second vowel in the team is shy. It stays silent.

3. **sail**

 **OR**

4. **coat**

 **OR**

Underline the vowel digraph and then circle the picture that matches the word.

5. **sweet**

 **OR**

6. **peas**

 **OR**

LONG VOWELS: COMPLETE THE WORDS

Sleepy Shang High spilled vowel digraphs all over the floor.

Help him tidy up by completing the words.

1.

email

(ai) | ea

2.

b

ee | oa

3.

wh___l

oa | ee

4.

b___t

ai | oa

LONG VOWELS: COMPLETE THE WORDS

Sleepy Shang High spilled vowel digraphs all over the floor.

Help him tidy up by completing the words:

5.

br____n

ai | ee

6.

r____d

ea | ai

7.

g____t

ue | oa

8.

t____

ie | oa

SAME LONG VOWEL SOUNDS

oi and **oy** are different spellings that make the same vowel sound

oi
c**oi**n

oi is often used at the
beginning or **middle** of a word

oy
t**oy**

oy is often used at the
end of a word

ow and **ou** are different spellings that make the same vowel sound

ou
h**ou**se

ou is often used at the
beginning or **middle** of a word

ow
c**ow**

ow is used at the **beginning**,
middle, or **end** of a word

or and **au** are different spellings that make the same vowel sound

or
h**or**n

or is used at the **beginning**,
middle, or **end** of a word

au
s**au**ce

au is often used at the
beginning or **middle** of a word

Complete the word!

1.  toy

(oy) | or

2. s_____l

ow | oi

3. j_____

ow | oy

4. t___let

oi | au

Complete the word!

5. h_____l

ow | or

6. cl_____d

ou | oi

7. _____l

or | ow

8. fl_____er

ow | oy

Complete the word!

9. _____ **tumn**

au | oi

10. **c** _____ **n**

or | oy

11. **st** _____ **m**

ow | or

12. **l** _____ **nch**

ou | au

Many long vowels have an **r** in them. These are sometimes called r-controlled vowels.

er, **ir**, and **ur** are different spellings that often make the same sound.

er
germ

ir
bird

ur
surf

ar and **or** make their own sounds.

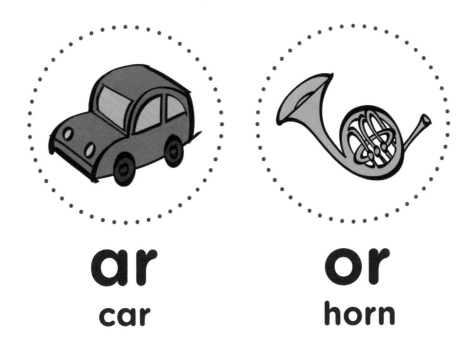

ar
car

or
horn

Yin and Yang go to a party!
They make lots of friends!

Help Yin and Yang describe their new friends.

Circle the word that best matches the picture.

1. (nurse) | curl

2. shark | farm

3. girl | thirsty

4. hurt | turkey

5. turtle | slurp

6. herd | germs

Oz wrote a list of everything
she wants for her birthday

But some of the letters are missing!

Complete the words to match the pictures.

1.

_jar

(ar) | er

2.

h____se

ur | or

3.

b____ger

ar | ur

4.

popc____n

or | ar

5.

sh____t

ir | or

6.

____t

ar | ur

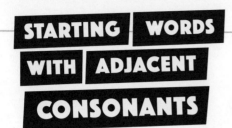

Adjacent consonants are two consonants that are next to each other in a word. This can make them harder to sound out and spell.

Sometimes these letters are called a consonant blend. You say each consonant quickly, so their sounds blend together.

Help Brick and Yang make an epic consonant blend smoothie!

Complete the word with a consonant blend to match the picture.

1.

_____ **cr ab**

dr (**cr**) **gr**

2.

ock

cl   fl   m

3.

_____anet

pl sn br

4.

_____arf

sp tw sc

5.

_____airs

st br tw

6.

_____ower

fl pl tr

7.

_____ake

tw fl sn

8.

_____ess

dr gr sk

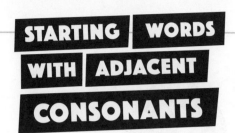

Adjacent consonants are two consonants that are next to each other in a word. This can make them harder to sound out and spell.

Sometimes these letters are called a consonant blend. You say each consonant quickly, so their sounds blend together.

Oz is making a movie! Help her choose which props to use.

Circle the word that matches the picture.

Underline the starting consonant blend.

1.

(**swing**) or **frog**

2.

stop or **star**

3.

snow or **spin**

4.

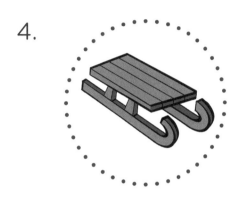

sleep or **sled**

5.

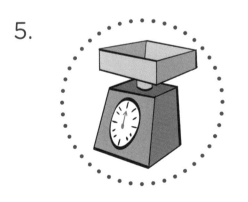

skate or **scale**

6.

frown or **crown**

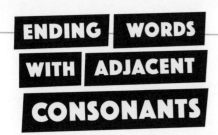

Adjacent consonants are two consonants that are next to each other in a word. This can make them harder to sound out and spell.

Sometimes these letters are called a consonant blend. You say each consonant quickly, so their sounds blend together.

Help Brick and Yang make an epic consonant blend smoothie!

Complete the word with a consonant blend to match the picture.

1.

po nd
----

mp (**nd**) **st**

2.

ba _____

nk **rn** **st**

3.

pai_____

lk   nt   ft

4.

toa_____

rm   nd   st

5.

la_____

mp   rf   nk

6.

ne_____

st   ld   nk

7.

e_____

ct   lf   fr

8.

ha_____

rt   rk   nd

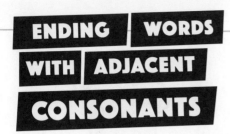

ENDING WORDS WITH ADJACENT CONSONANTS

Adjacent consonants are two consonants that are next to each other in a word. This can make them harder to sound out and spell.

Sometimes these letters are called a consonant blend. You say each consonant quickly, so their sounds blend together.

Oz is making a movie! Help her choose which props to use.

Circle the word that matches the picture.

Underline the ending consonant blend.

1.

(**stamp**) or **sink**

2.

sand or **band**

3.

test or **tent**

4.

golf or **gold**

5.

lift or **gift**

6.

toast or **boast**

Words are made up of sounds. Some words end with the same sounds. These words rhyme.

Circle the picture that rhymes with the word.

1. **sing**

2. **fell**

3. **rock**

4. **wall**

5. **look**

Circle the word that does not rhyme with the other words.

1.   **three**   **tree**   (**wash**)

2.   **red**   **bag**   **bed**

3.   **pot**   **sun**   **fun**

4.   **bug**   **star**   **mug**

5.   **fish**   **dish**   **lock**

Words are made up of sounds. Some words end with the same sounds. These words rhyme.

Complete the poem with the word that rhymes.

Row, row, row your boat, gently down the stream.

If you see a crocodile, don't forget to _____ **!**

shout   **scream**

Three little monkeys
jumping on the bed,

One fell down and
bumped
his _____ .

head   foot

Mama called the
doctor and the
doctor said,

"No more monkeys
jumping on
the _____ !"

grass   bed

COMMON ENDINGS ang, ing, ong, ung!

Big Ben is broken! It goes "ang ing ong ung!"

Sometimes, you have to remember to say the letters at the end of a word differently. You say all the letter sounds, but in a faster and stickier way, like ang, ing, ong, and ung. These are sometimes called glued sounds.

Underline the glued endings. Circle the word that matches the picture.

1.

(ring) | sung

2.

lung | wrong

3.

hang | sing

4.

fang | king

5.

wing | thing

6.

long | dung

7.

gong | swing

8.

song | bang

9.

sting | bring

10.

strong | string

PHONICS:
SOUND BUTTONS &
READING PRACTICE

1. Sound button the words.

When a single letter (grapheme) makes one sound (phoneme), put a **dot** under it.

cat
. . .

Spot the digraphs or trigraphs and **underline** them.

night   tail   chat
. — .   . — .   — — . .

2. Blend and read the words.

1.	**feel**	2.	**book**
3.	**rain**	4.	**night**
5.	**feet**	6.	**tool**
7.	**near**	8.	**wail**

78

9. **soak**

10. **look**

11. **sail**

12. **right**

13. **moon**

14. **boat**

15. **fight**

16. **seem**

Try to decode these non-real words in the same way.

17. **zook**

18. **naim**

19. **beem**

20. **jight**

PHONICS:
SOUND BUTTONS & READING PRACTICE

INSTRUCTIONS:

1. Sound button the words.

When a single letter (grapheme) makes one sound (phoneme), put a **dot** under it.

cat
• • •

Spot the digraphs or trigraphs and **underline** them.

night   tail   chat
• _ _ •   • _ •   _ • •

2. Blend and read the words.

3. Real or not real?

On this page there are words that are real and words that are not real. You have to decide which is which.

Tick the box if the word is **real**.

cat ✓   pag ☐
• • •   • • •

1. **gilk** ☐   2. **clap** ☐

3. **bleed** ☐   4. **spait** ☐

5. **freeg** ☐   6. **pump** ☐

7.	**coach**	☐
9.	**float**	☐
11.	**sand**	☐
13.	**throat**	☐
15.	**truck**	☐
17.	**creek**	☐

8.	**crab**	☐
10.	**rant**	☐
12.	**list**	☐
14.	**bink**	☐
16.	**lift**	☐
18.	**deed**	☐

INSTRUCTIONS:

1. Sound button the words.

When a single letter (grapheme) makes one sound (phoneme), put a **dot** under it.

cat

Spot the digraphs or trigraphs and **underline** them.

night   tail   chat

2. Blend and read the words.

1. **insect**

2. **invent**

3. **sleeping**

4. **napkin**

5. **painting**

6. **sickness**

82

7. **fishing**

8. **backpack**

9. **feeling**

10. **airbus**

11. **darkness**

12. **unless**

13. **family**

14. **habit**

Try to decode these non-real words in the same way.

15. **femely**

16. **exun**

17. **ganrock**

18. **grinit**

PHONICS:
SOUND BUTTONS &
READING PRACTICE

1. Sound button the words.

When a single letter (grapheme) makes one sound (phoneme), put a **dot** under it.

cat
• • •

Spot the digraphs or trigraphs and **underline** them.

night tail chat

Spot the vowel teams with final **-e** (split digraphs) and connect them.

cake

2. Blend and read the words.

3. Real or not real?

On this page there are words that are real and words that are not real. You have to decide which is which.

Tick the box if the word is **real**.

cat   pag ☐
• • •   • • •

1. **herb** ☐

2. **germ** ☐

3. **star** ☐

4. **whuck** ☐

5. **glane** ☐

6. **care** ☐

7. **gife** ☐

8. **dare** ☐

9. **key** ☐

10. **more** ☐

11. **feal** ☐

12. **roink** ☐

13. **slow** ☐

14. **shake** ☐

15. **bird** ☐

16. **bark** ☐

17. **term** ☐

18. **lie** ☐

PHONICS:
SOUND BUTTONS &
READING PRACTICE

INSTRUCTIONS:

1. **Sound button the words.**

When a single letter (grapheme) makes one sound (phoneme), put a **dot** under it.

cat

Spot the digraphs or trigraphs and **underline** them.

night   tail   chat

Spot the vowel teams with final **-e** (split digraphs) and connect them.

cake

2. **Blend and read the words.**

Remember to blend and read each syllable first and then the whole word.

1.	**athlete**	2.	**needy**
3.	**messy**	4.	**delete**
5.	**meeting**	6.	**cheeky**

7. **sleepy**

8. **complete**

9. **songbird**

10. **flying**

11. **dirty**

12. **thirteen**

13. **fairly**

14. **concrete**

Try to decode these non-real words in the same way.

15. **keady**

16. **reedful**

17. **greeming**

18. **coateen**

VOCABULARY

BIG & SMALL

A synonym is a word that means the same as
another word. These are synonyms of big.

These mean big, very big, and
very, very big.

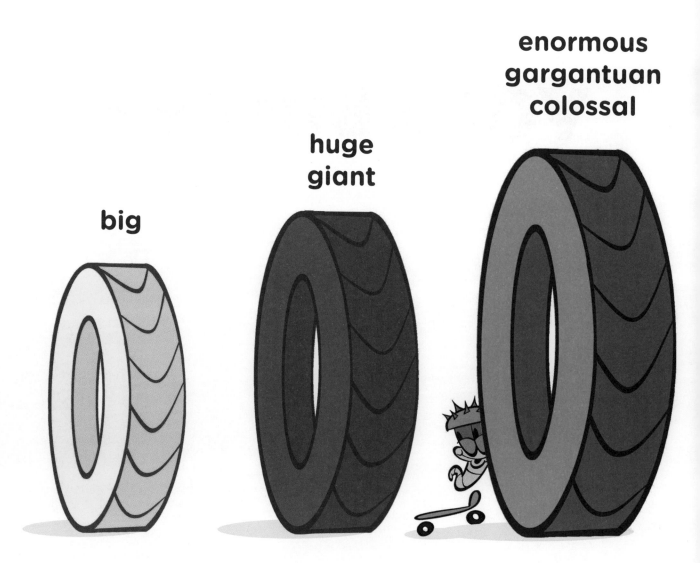

enormous
gargantuan
colossal

huge
giant

big

An antonym is a word that means the opposite of another word. These are antonyms of big.

These mean small, very small, and very, very small.

small

tiny

**minuscule
microscopic**

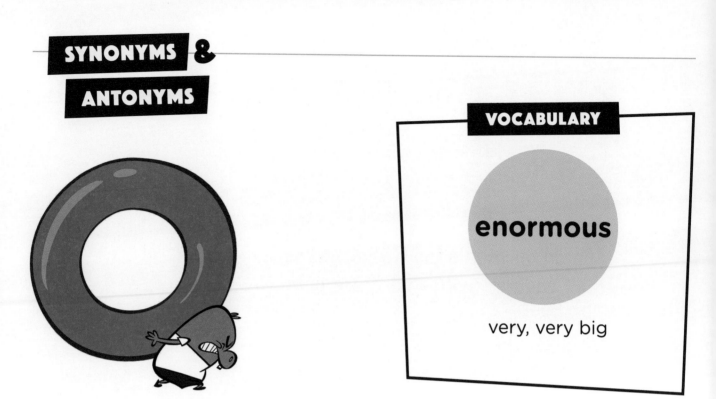

enormous

very, very big

Circle the words that mean the same as **big**.

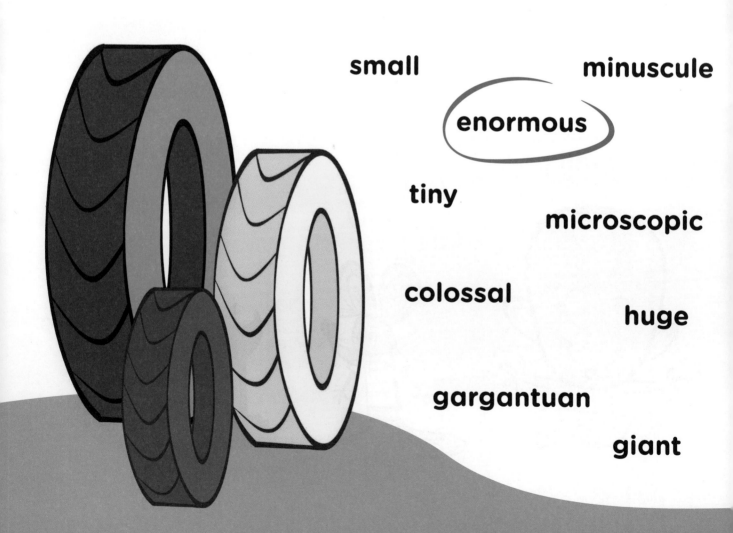

small

minuscule

enormous

tiny

microscopic

colossal

huge

gargantuan

giant

HAPPY & SAD

A synonym is a word that means the same as another word. These are synonyms of happy.

These mean happy, very happy, and very, very happy.

happy

delighted

overjoyed
ecstatic

HAPPY & SAD

An antonym is a word that means the opposite of another word. These are antonyms of happy.

These mean sad, very sad,
and very, very sad.

sad

upset
melancholy

heartbroken

ecstatic

very, very happy

Circle the words that mean the same as **happy**.

delighted

melancholy

upset

heartbroken

overjoyed

ecstatic

sad

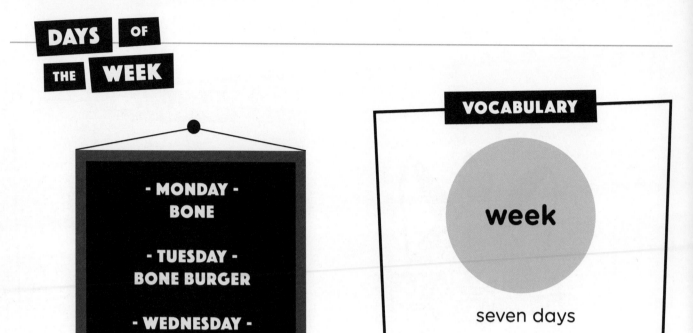

- MONDAY -
BONE

- TUESDAY -
BONE BURGER

- WEDNESDAY -
BONES ON TOAST

VOCABULARY

week

seven days

Look at the specials board and write the correct days of the week in the gaps!

1. _____ Monday _____

2. -----------------------------------

3. -----------------------------------

4.

THURSDAY
CHICKENLESS BONE
BUCKET

- FRIDAY -
SUPERSIZE BONE

- SATURDAY -
BONE CONE

- SUNDAY -
BASIC BONE BROTH

Thursday

5.

6.

7.

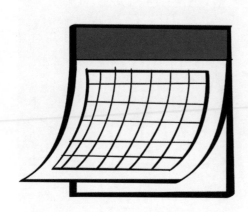

Choose the correct months of the year and write them in the gaps!

J̲anuary̲

F_____

M_____

A_____

M_____

J_____

June   October   August

September   April   February

May   January   March

November   December   July

J u l y _____   A _____   S _____

O _____   N _____   D _____

PUT THE WORDS IN ALPHABETICAL ORDER

Grit is opening an ice cream shop!
Help him design his dream menu.

Put the words below in alphabetical order. This means put them in the order that their first letters appear in the alphabet.

strawberry   **mint**   **lemon**   **coconut**

orange   **blueberry**   **grape**   **vanilla**

1. blueberry   2. _____   3. _____

4. _____   5. _____   6. _____

7. _____   8. _____

Uh oh... there has been a messy mistake!
There's paint everywhere!

Help the characters clean up by naming all the paints.

**blue | red | green | purple
yellow | white | pink**

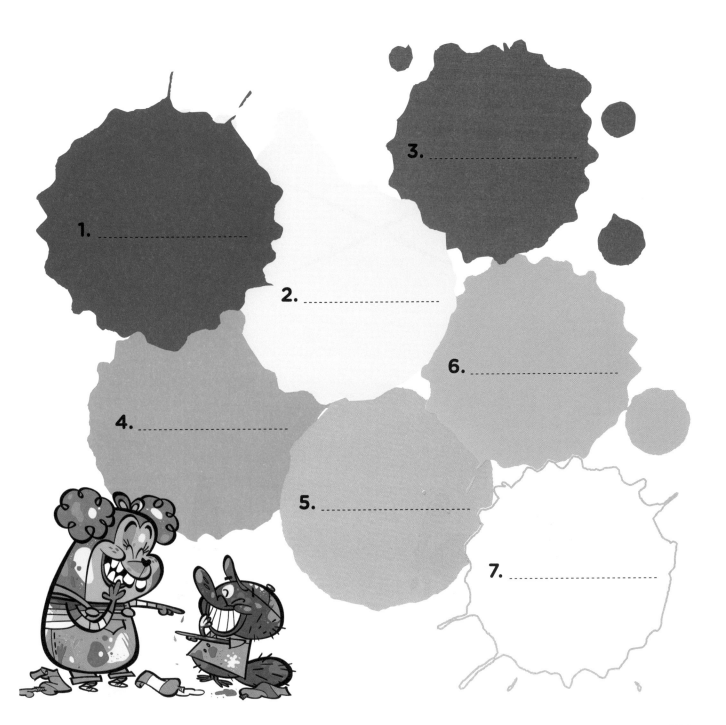

1. ----------------------

2. ----------------------

3. ----------------------

4. ----------------------

5. ----------------------

6. ----------------------

7. ----------------------

WORDS WITH
MULTIPLE MEANINGS

Some words look the same but have different meanings. Bark is the noise that dogs make and the outside part of a tree.

Match the sentences to the pictures.
Draw a line to connect them.

1. The bells ring.   She is wearing a ring.

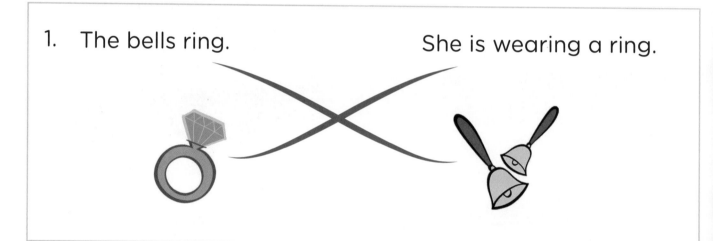

2. I hit the ball with my bat.   The bat can fly.

3. He is a fan of sport!   The fan kept them cool.

4. He has a cold.   It is cold outside.

5. She waves with both arms.   The ocean waves are strong.

GRAMMAR

sit

is a **verb**.

A verb is all about doing or being.
Often, they are action words like sit, eat, and laugh.

Circle the verbs on this page!

jump

sit

hairy

lemon

be

think

magnet

draw

taste

106

VOCABULARY

scarf is a **noun**.

A noun is a person, place, or thing, like Armie, Earth, and scarf.

Circle the nouns on this page!

scarf

tree

little

Oz

paint

house

tired

yellow

beach

VOCABULARY

loud

is an **adjective**.

An adjective is a describing word.
It describes a noun, like <u>loud</u> music.

Circle the adjectives on this page!

quiet

ball

carrot

swim

tired

blue

hot   frozen

ACTION VERBS

A verb is a word that tells you what someone is doing.
An action verb is a verb that describes an action,
like run or smile.

Choose the action verb that best describes the picture. Write the verbs in the gaps.

ACTION WORDS

1. Swim

2.

3.

4.

- sleep
- read
- kick
- swim

109

Prepositions tell you where something
is or where something happens.

Write the prepositions next to the matching picture.

1.

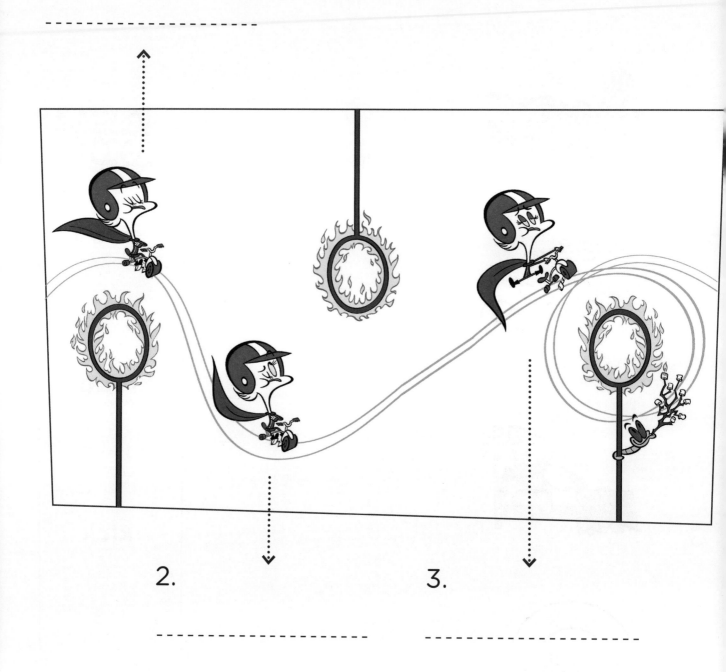

2.

3.

under | **around** | **over**

4.

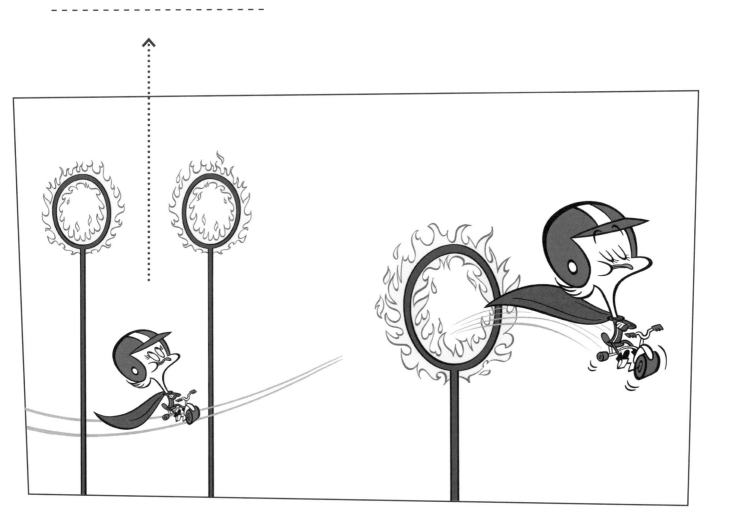

5.

through | **between**

CONJUNCTIONS

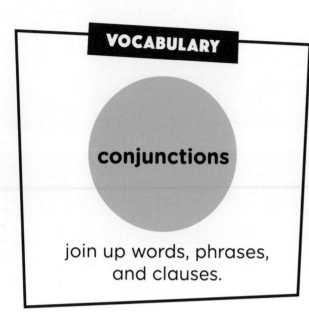

conjunctions

join up words, phrases, and clauses.

Complete the sentences below with the correct conjunction.

and	but	because	so

1. Plato made a strawberry _____and_____ banana smoothie.

2. Bearnice was tired _____ she went to bed.

3. Bogart was late _____ he missed the bus.

4. Oz doesn't like to sing, _____ she likes to dance.

PLURALS -S AND -ES

To make a noun plural you can:
Add -s to most nouns or add -es, if the
noun ends in -s, -ch, -sh, -x, or -z.

Write out these plural nouns.

1. **tree + s =** _trees_

2. **hand + s =** _____

3. **fox + es =** _____

4. **glass + es =** _____

5. **goat + s =** _____

6. **wish + es =** _____

7. **house + s =** _____

8. **beach + es =** _____

IRREGULAR PLURALS

Circle the word that matches the picture.

1.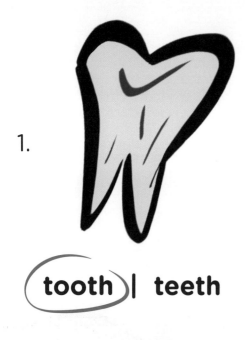

(tooth) | **teeth**

2.

mice | **mouse**

3.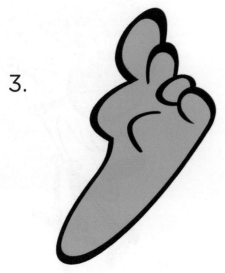

feet | **foot**

4.

children | **child**

5.

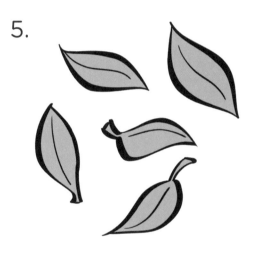

leaves | leaf

6.

geese | goose

7.

wolf | wolves

Every sentence ends with
an end mark.

This is a **period** or **full stop**. It comes at the end of a sentence.

This is a **question mark**. It comes at the end of a question.

This is an **exclamation mark**. It comes at the end of a sentence that shows a strong feeling.

Draw a line to match the
end marks to their names.

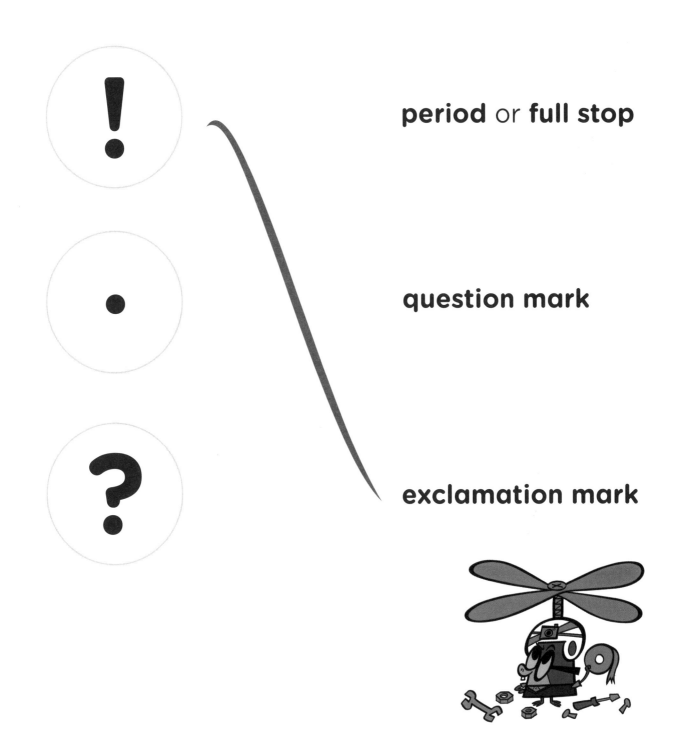

!

.

?

period or **full stop**

question mark

exclamation mark

SENTENCE TYPES

A statement tells something. It ends with a full stop.

I am hungry.

A question asks something that needs an answer. It ends with a question mark.

When is lunch?

STATEMENTS

Circle the statements.

1   (Oz is a singer.)   Does Oz love to paint?

2   Is Plato a chef?   Plato is a chef.

3   Yin ate her dinner.   What did Yin eat
                               for dinner?

4   When did Bearnice   Bearnice went to bed.
    go to bed?

5   Did Grit brush his teeth? Grit brushed his teeth.

IMPERATIVES

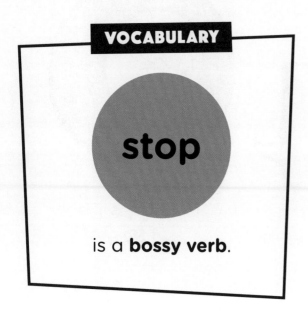

stop

is a **bossy verb**.

Imperatives are bossy verbs — they tell you what to do.

They go at the start of a sentence
to turn it into a command.

Make these sentences bossy!
The first one is done for you.

1. Please could you stop drawing on the walls?

   Stop drawing on the walls!

2. I would like you to make my dinner.

3. Would you please read me a story?

Questions often start with a question word.

Who? To ask about a person.
What? To ask about a thing.
When? To ask about a time.
Where? To ask about a place.
Why? To ask for a reason.

Pick the right question word and write it in the gap.

1.   Who   ate the cake?   Who | When

2. _____ is your birthday?   When | Why

3. _____ do you live?   What | Where

4. _____ is fire hot?   Why | Who

5. _____ is your new teacher?   Who | When

6. _____ is in your bag?   Why | What

HIGH-FREQUENCY WORDS

Use the paint by words chart to complete the picture and find the hidden words. Use crayons, pencils, or paint!

BLUE **just**

RED **from**

GREEN **day**

ORANGE **it's**

YELLOW **don't**

When you've found them all, colour the rest of the picture.

MATHS CONCEPTS & VOCABULARY

EVEN NUMBERS

VOCABULARY

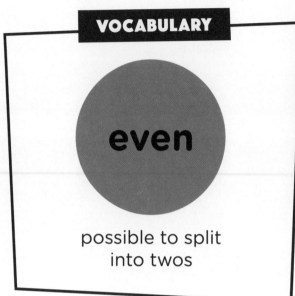

even

possible to split into twos

How many gloves? Count the even number of gloves and write it in the gap.

1.

_2_

two

2.

3.

4.

5.

ODD NUMBERS

odd

impossible to split into twos

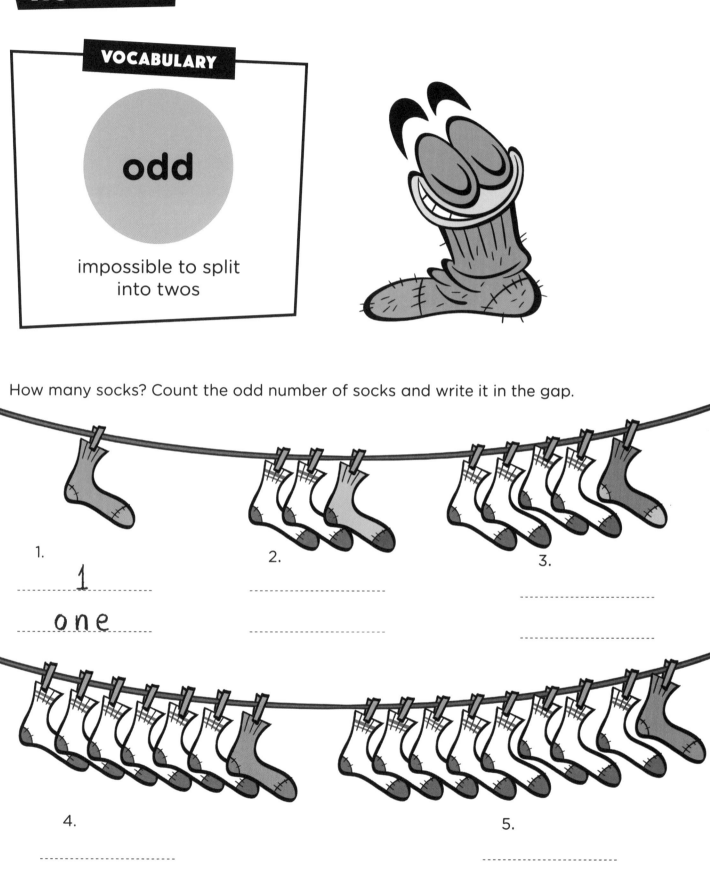

How many socks? Count the odd number of socks and write it in the gap.

1.

_____1_____

___one___

2.

3.

4.

5.

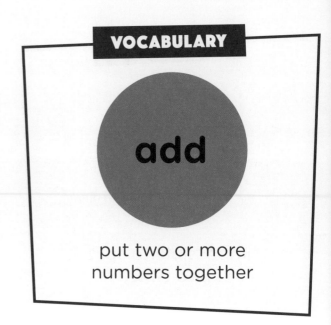

Add up the cookies! Write your answers in the gaps.

one plus one equals...

1.  1 +  1 =  2

two plus two equals...

2.  ------- +  ------- =  -------

four plus four equals...

3.  ------- +  ------- =  -------

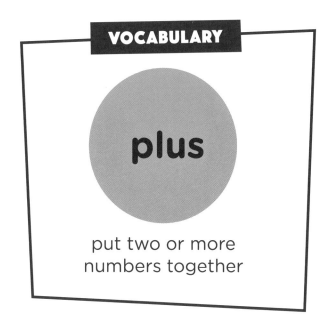

4.   A cat has five toes on its front paws and four toes on its back paws. Add them up!

5 + 5 + 4 + 4 = _18_

5.   A platypus has five toes on each of its four webbed feet. Add them up!

5 + 5 + 5 + 5 = _____

6. An ostrich has two toes on each of its two feet. Add them up!

2 + 2 = _____

7. A hippo has four toes on each of its four feet. Add them up!

4 + 4 + 4 + 4 = _____

VOCABULARY

add

put two or more
numbers together

8. A giraffe has two toes on each of its four feet. Add them up!

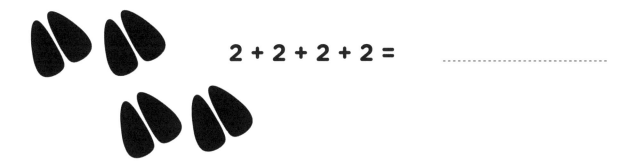

$2 + 2 + 2 + 2 =$ _____

9. And finally, how many toes do worms have?

_____

**subtract
or minus**

take a number away
from another

Subtract the cookies! Write your answers in the gaps.

two minus one equals...

1.  2 -  1 = 1

four minus two equals...

2.  -  =

eight minus four equals...

3.  -  =

NUMBER BONDS

VOCABULARY

number bond

a pair of numbers that add up to another number

Use the stack of tyres to help you complete the number bonds.

1. _____1_____ + _____9_____ = 10

2. _____ + _____ = 10

3. _____ + _____ = 10

4. _____ + _____ = 10

5. _____ + _____ = 10

SKIP-COUNTING BY TWOS

counting in twos

Count the cheeks full of cookies! Write the numbers in the gaps.

1.

<u> 2 </u>

<u>two</u>

3.

2.

_____

_____

4.

_____

_____

5.

_____

_____

Keep going!

6.

12
twelve

8.

7.

9.

10.

There are five doughnuts in each box. Write how many doughnuts Plato eats in the gaps!

1. ____5____
five

2.

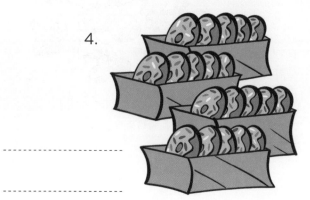

_____

_____

3. _____

_____

4.

_____

_____

5.

_____

_____

6.
30
thirty

7.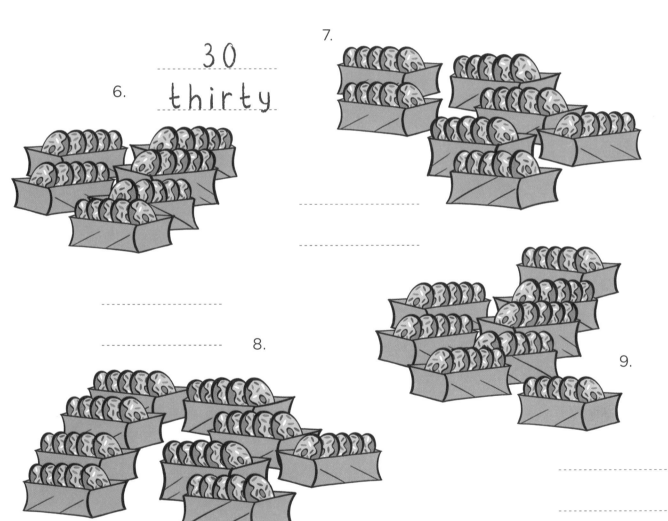

8.

9.

SKIP-COUNTING BY TENS

counting in tens

There are 10 bees in each family. How many bees are in each swarm?
Write the numbers in the gaps!

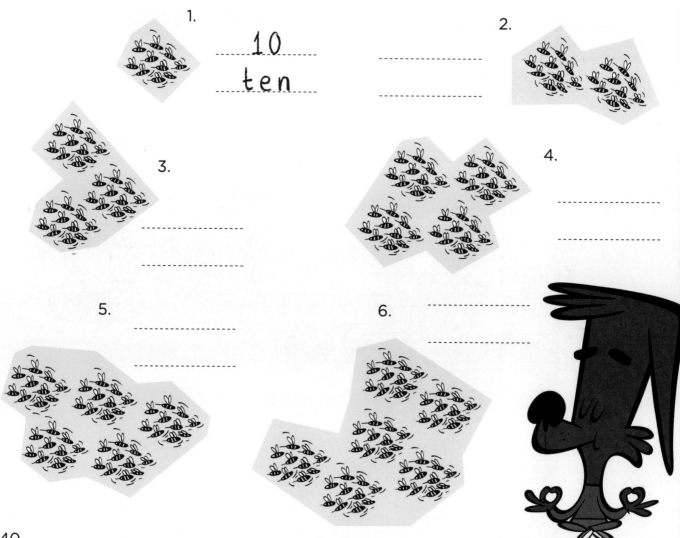

1.
10
ten

2.

3.

4.

5.

6.

I can't sleep!

Help Shang High fall
asleep by counting the sheep.

Write the number words in the gaps.

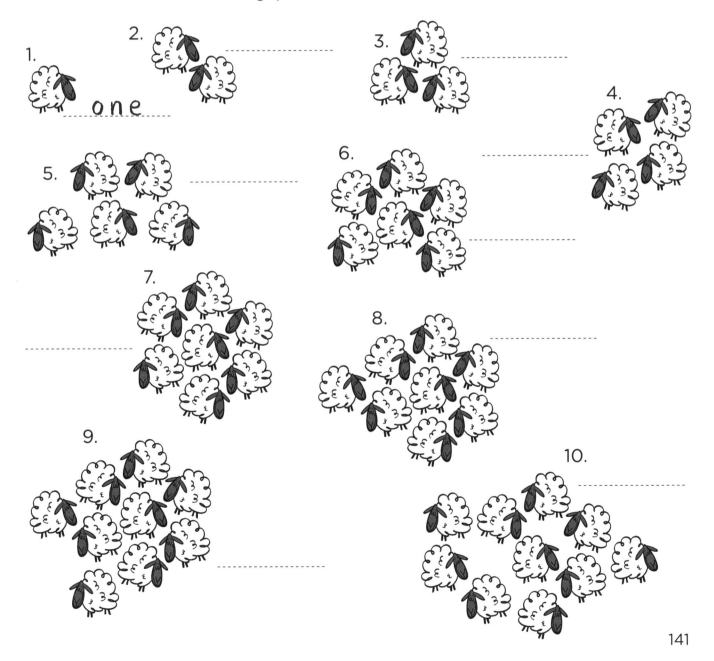

1.

one

2.

3.

4.

5.

6.

7.

8.

9.

10.

share

to use or enjoy
something with others

10 mm
1 cm

25 mm
2.5 cm

150 mm
15 cm

Use your hotdog ruler to measure these things in your kitchen in centimetres!

a carrot

a jar

a fork

----------- cm

----------- cm

----------- cm

MEASURING IN FEET

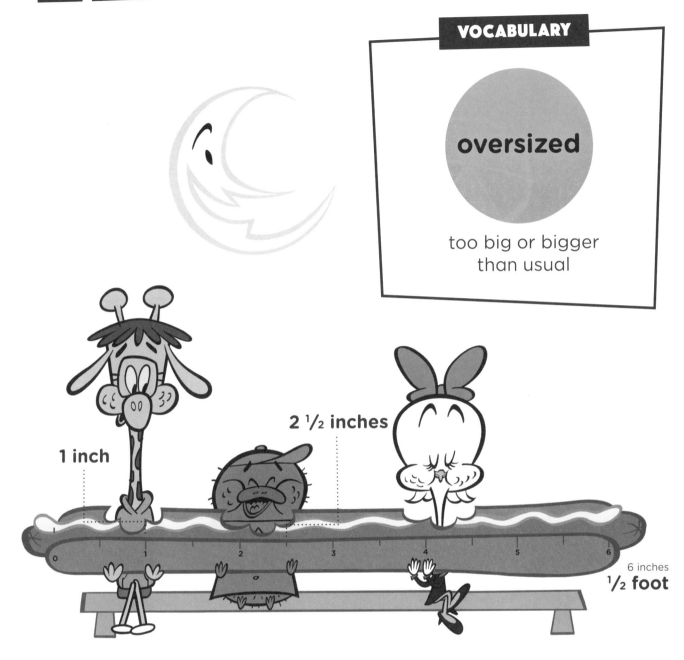

1 inch

2 ½ inches

6 inches
½ foot

Now use your hotdog ruler to measure these things in inches!

a glass

a slice of bread

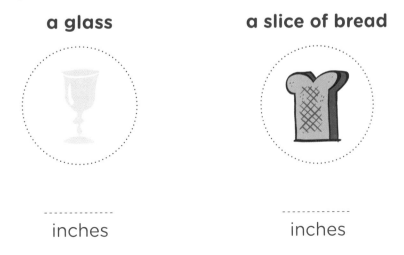

----
inches

----
inches

Not to scale

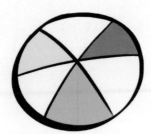

height

how tall or high something is from top to bottom

How many feet tall is the wave that Armie is surfing?

50 ft

45 ft

40 ft

35 ft

30 ft

25 ft

20 ft

15 ft

10 ft

144

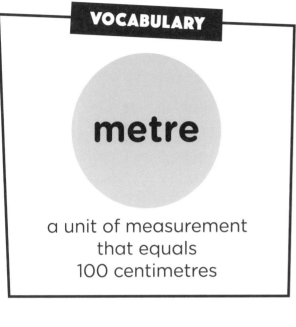

VOCABULARY

metre

a unit of measurement that equals 100 centimetres

How many metres tall is the wave that Armie is surfing?

50 m

45 m

40 m

35 m

30 m

25 m

20 m

15 m

10 m

UNDERSTANDING BAR CHARTS

How many glasses of water should each age group drink per day?
Read the chart and write the numbers in the gaps!

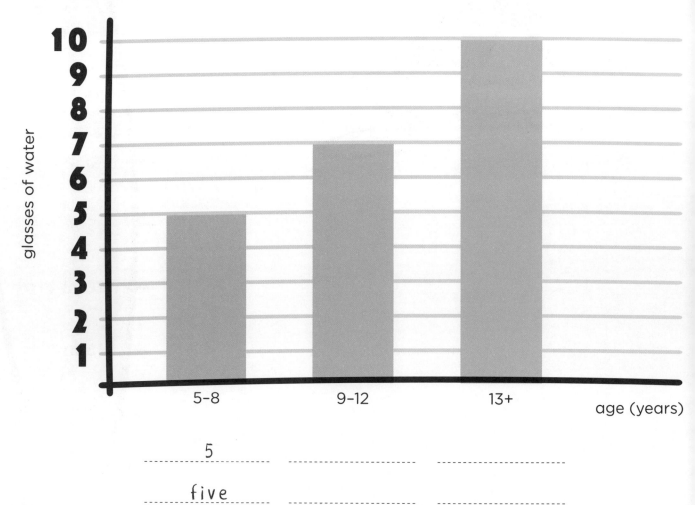

glasses of water

10
9
8
7
6
5
4
3
2
1

| 5-8 | 9-12 | 13+ |

age (years)

5

five

146

3D SHAPES

3D shapes

three dimensional - solid!

Can you match the 3D shapes to the objects?
Draw a line with your pencil!

1. cone

2. cylinder

3. sphere

4. cube

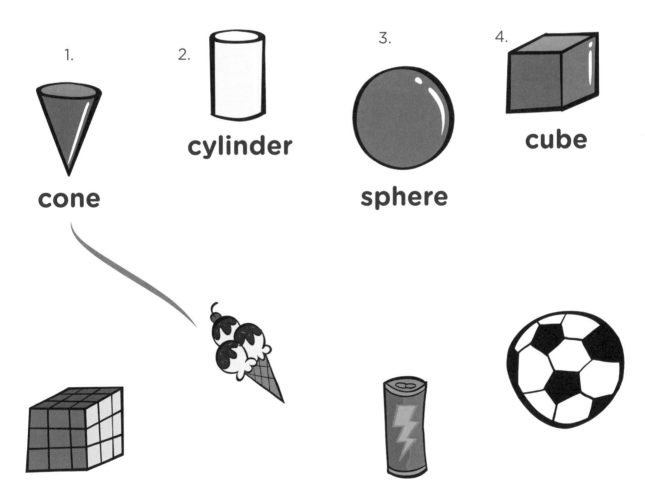

ADDING UP: MONEY

VOCABULARY

money

what you use to buy stuff

Look at today's menu.
Write down how much
it will cost to order:

TODAY'S MENU

tacos · 10

kiwi juice · 5

burritos · 10

doughnut · 2

guacamole · 5

1. **One taco and one kiwi juice?**

   £15

   fifteen pounds

2. **Two doughnuts?**

   _____

   _____

3. **Two burritos and one guacamole?**

   _____

   _____

4. **One of everything on the menu?**

   _____

   _____

148

SECONDS TO MINUTES

BRUSH YOUR TEETH FOR 2 MINUTES

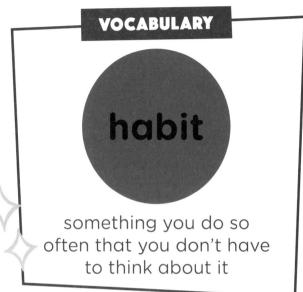
How long is Grit brushing his teeth for?
Write your answers in the gaps!

120 seconds

2. _____
minutes

180 seconds

3. _____
minutes

60 seconds

1. ___1___

minute

VOCABULARY

screen time

the amount of time you spend looking at a device

Ask everyone in your family how long they think they spend looking at devices every day.

Name	Time looking at devices (hours and minutes)
....	....
....	....
....	....
....	....
....	....
....	....

Now add them up! In total, how long does your family spend looking at screens?

.... **hours**

.... **minutes**

TELLING TIME

Grit forgot to set his alarm clock! Look at the clocks and write the times.

1.

s e v e n **o'clock**

7:00

2.

_____ **o'clock**

_____

3.

_____ **o'clock**

_____

4.

_____ **o'clock**

_____

5.

_____ **o'clock**

_____

VOCABULARY

VOCABULARY

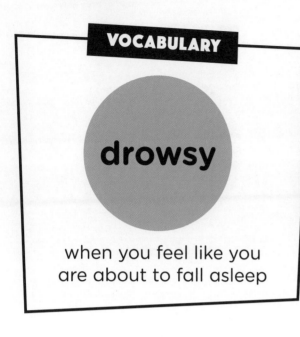

drowsy

when you feel like you
are about to fall asleep

Looks like it's time for Yin and Yang's nap! Look at the clocks and write the times.

6.

half past two **o'clock**

2:30

7.

_____ **o'clock**

8.

_____ **o'clock**

_____

9.

_____ **o'clock**

_____

10.

_____ **o'clock**

_____

VOCABULARY

exhausted

when you are very tired
and worn out

How late did Shang High go to bed? He's exhausted!
Look at the clocks and write the times.

11.

half past eleven **o'clock**

11:30

13.

o'clock

12.

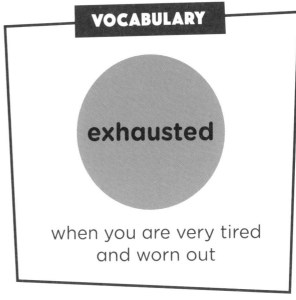

o'clock

14.

o'clock

15.

o'clock

LISTENING, SPEAKING, CREATING

ALL ABOUT ME-MOJI

HI! MY NAME IS

_____

Draw your me-moji:

I AM

_____

YEARS OLD

♥ **THIS IS MY FAMILY** ♥

MY FRIENDS ARE

 _____

 _____

 _____

_____

Circle a me-moji that shows how you feel.

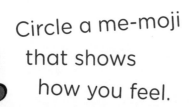

HAPPY

CONFUSED

SAD

SILLY

MISCHIEVOUS

MY FAVOURITE:

food

colour

sport

book

video game

TV show

If I could have any pet in the world, it would be a...

Draw what you think will happen as a result of the first image.
Write a sentence to show what happened under both images.

CAUSE:

What happened first?

EFFECT:

What happened as a result?

Cause and effect show how two events are related.
The second event (effect) happens as a result of
the first event (cause).

CAUSE & EFFECT

Draw what you think will happen as a result of the first image.
Write a sentence to show what happened under both images.

CAUSE:

What happened first?

EFFECT:

What happened as a result?

Cause and effect show how two events are related.
The second event (effect) happens as a result of
the first event (cause).

CAUSE & EFFECT

Draw what you think happened first.
Write a sentence to show what happened under both images.

CAUSE:

What happened first?

What happened as a result?

....

....

Cause and effect show how two events are related.
The second event (effect) happens as a result of
the first event (cause).

SEQUENCING

Write **1** in the circle to show what happened **first**. Write **2** in the circle to show what happened **next**. Write **3** in the circle to show what happened **last**. Write a sentence next to each image to explain what is happening.

Colour in the picture!

NOTHING IS BEYOND YOUR REACH.

1. Trace the words.

2. Try it out. Start with Bogart's emoji.

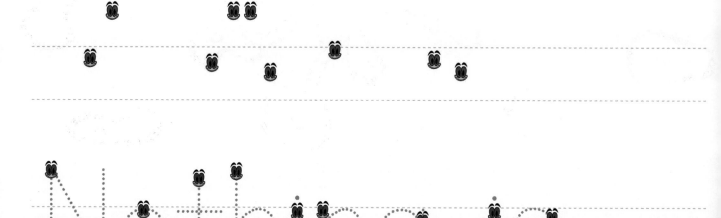

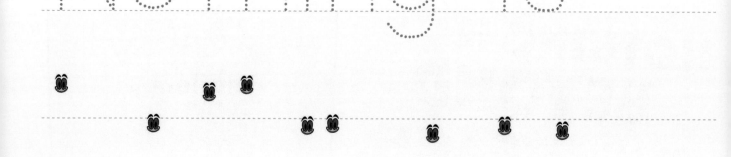

beyond

your

reach.

169

Colour in the picture!

REMEMBER, FEELINGS COME AND GO.

mindful

focusing on the present moment

1. Trace the words.

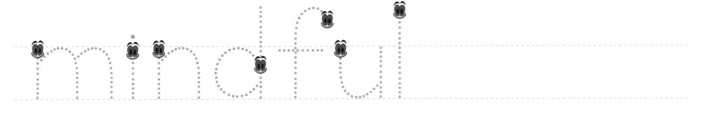

2. Try it out. Start with Bogart's emoji.

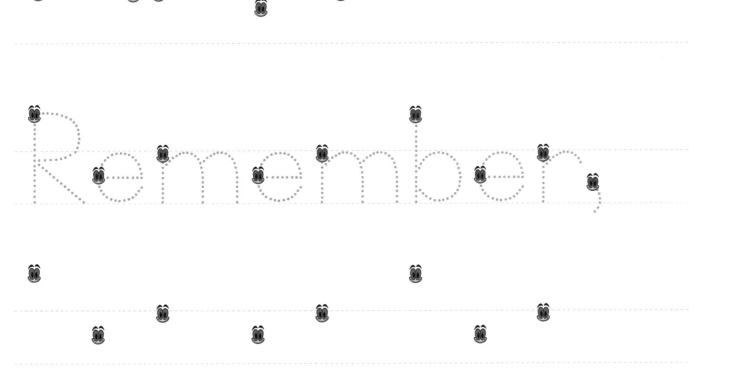

feelings

come

and go.

Colour in the picture!

COLLECT MEMORIES, NOT THINGS.

friends

people who get along
well and love each other

1. Trace the words.

friends

2. Try it out. Start with Bogart's emoji.

Collect

memories

not

things.

TEDDY Talks: 3D PRINTING

Teddy Talks are about creating something new and sharing it with the world!

design

plan to make something

Oz is using a 3D printer to make a new teddy bear. A 3D printer prints thousands of tiny slices of plastic that fit together like a puzzle. Then, it stacks these slices like pancakes to make a solid object like a teddy bear!

Now that you have all the answers,
give a Teddy Talk about them!

3D-lite

PRINTER

1. **What is a 3D printer?**

2. **How does it work?**

3. **What would you make in a printer?**

1. Write your notes here.

2. Draw a picture to show someone.

TEDDY Talks:

HOW TO TIE YOUR SHOES

Teddy Talks are about creating something new and sharing it with the world!

VOCABULARY

understand

know how or why something works

Look at the instructions for how to tie your shoes in five easy steps.
Make sure you remember them all!

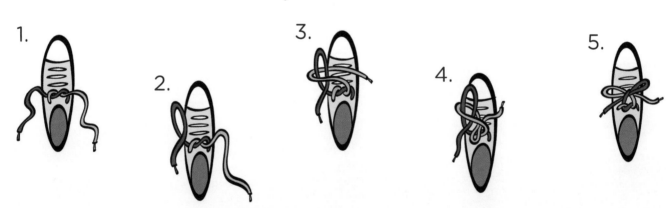

1. 2. 3. 4. 5.

Now, give a Teddy Talk to your family and friends,
explaining how to tie your shoes!

1. What are shoes?

2. Why do we need to tie them?

3. What's the first step?

4. What's the final step?

1. Write your notes here.

TEDDY Talks:

DESIGN YOUR OWN HOVERBOARD

Teddy Talks are about creating something new and sharing it with the world!

VOCABULARY

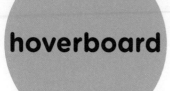

hoverboard

a mode of transport you stand on that floats above the ground

What's even more exciting than a scooter? A hoverboard! Design yours on the next page and make a list of some of its best features.

1. Design your own hoverboard here.

2. What are your hoverboard's best features?

PAGE 19

rain – L

cat – S

paint – L

egg – S

feet – L

bed – S

night – L

pig – S

milk – S

mop – S

goat – L

boat – L

duck – S

boot – L

sun – S

PAGE 20

1. **paint - long vowel**

2. **cat - short vowel**

3. **rain - long vowel**

4. **ant - short vowel**

PAGE 21

1. **sheep - long vowel**

2. **feet - long vowel**

3. **nest - short vowel**

4. **red - short vowel**

PAGE 22

1. **fish - short vowel**

2. **ring - short vowel**

3. **night - long vowel**

4. **light - long vowel**

PAGE 23

1. **toad - long vowel**

2. **box - short vowel**

3. **toast - long vowel**

4. **dog - short vowel**

PAGE 24

1. **sun - short vowel**

2. **food - long vowel**

3. **shampoo - long vowel**

4. **bug - short vowel**

PAGE 25

Short vowels: **bag milk frog ant sun**
Long vowels: **soap room high sail bee**

PAGE 36-37

Short vowels: **map hat man plum duck**
Long vowels: **feet coin night tree join**

Short vowels: **hot mop stuck cap kit**
Long vowels: **point moon tooth queen tail**

PAGE 49-51

Page 49
1. **cape**
2. **cane**

Page 50
3. **kite**
4. **robe**

Page 51
5. **cube**
6. **tape**
7. **cute**
8. **hate**

PAGE 52-54

1. t**oa**d
2. b**ea**ch
3. s**ai**l
4. c**oa**t
5. sw**ee**t
6. p**ea**s

PAGE 55-56

1. em**ai**l
2. b**ee**
3. wh**ee**l
4. b**oa**t
5. br**ai**n
6. r**ea**d
7. g**oa**t
8. ti**e**

PAGE 58-59

1. t**oy**
2. s**oil**
3. j**oy**
4. t**oi**let
5. h**owl**
6. cl**ou**d
7. **owl**
8. fl**ow**er

PAGE 60

9. **au**tumn
10. c**or**n
11. st**or**m
12. l**au**nch

PAGE 62-63

1. n**ur**se
2. sh**ar**k
3. th**ir**sty
4. h**ur**t
5. t**ur**tle
6. g**er**ms

1. j**ar**
2. h**or**se
3. b**ur**ger
4. popc**or**n
5. sh**ir**t
6. **ar**t

PAGE 80-81

Not real words:

1. gilk

4. spait

5. freeg

14. bink

PAGE 84-85

Not real words:

4. whuck

5. glane

7. gife

11. feal

12. roink

PAGE 92

huge

giant

enormous

gargantuan

colossal

PAGE 95

delighted

overjoyed

ecstatic

PAGE 96-97

1. Monday

2. Tuesday

3. Wednesday

4. Thursday

5. Friday

6. Saturday

7. Sunday

PAGE 98-99

January
February
March
April
May
June

July
August
September
October
November
December

PAGE 100

1. blueberry

2. coconut

3. grape

4. lemon

5. mint

6. orange

7. strawberry

8. vanilla

PAGE 101

1. purple

2. yellow

3. red

4. green

5. blue

6. pink

7. white

1. The bells ring. =
   She is wearing a ring. =

2. I hit the ball with my bat. =
   The bat can fly. =

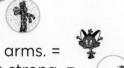

3. He is a fan of sport! =
   The fan kept them cool. =

4. He has a cold. =
   It is cold outside. =

5. She waves with both arms. =
   The ocean waves are strong. =

Verbs: sit, jump, taste, be, think, draw

Nouns: scarf, tree, Oz, house, paint, beach

Adjectives: loud, quiet, tired, blue, hot, frozen

1. swim

2. kick

3. sleep

4. read

1. over   4. between

2. under   5. through

3. around

1. and

2. so

3. because

4. but

1. trees   5. goats

2. hands   6. wishes

3. foxes   7. houses

4. glasses   8. beaches

1. tooth   5. leaves

2. mice   6. goose

3. foot   7. wolf

4. child

PAGE 117

! exclamation mark

? question mark

. period or full stop

PAGE 119

1. Oz is a singer.

2. Plato is a chef.

3. Yin ate her dinner.

4. Bearnice went to bed.

5. Grit brushed his teeth.

PAGE 120

1. Stop drawing on the walls!

2. Make my dinner!

3. Read me a story!

PAGE 121

1. **Who** ate the cake?

2. **When** is your birthday?

3. **Where** do you live?

4. **Why** is fire hot?

5. **Who** is your new teacher?

6. **What** is in your bag?

PAGE 128–129

1. 2, two
2. 4, four
3. 6, six
4. 8, eight
5. 10, ten

1. 1, one
2. 3, three
3. 5, five
4. 7, seven
5. 9, nine

PAGE 130–133

1. $1 + 1 = 2$

2. $2 + 2 = 4$

3. $4 + 4 = 8$

4. 18

5. 20

6. 4

7. 16

8. 8

9. 0

PAGE 134

1. $2 - 1 = 1$

2. $4 - 2 = 2$

3. $8 - 4 = 4$

PAGE 135

1. $1 + 9 = 10$

2. $4 + 6 = 10$

3. $5 + 5 = 10$

4. $3 + 7 = 10$

5. $2 + 8 = 10$

PAGE 136–137

1. 2, two
2. 4, four
3. 6, six
4. 8, eight
5. 10, ten
6. 12, twelve
7. 14, fourteen
8. 16, sixteen
9. 18, eighteen
10. 20, twenty

PAGE 138–139

1. 5, five
2. 10, ten
3. 15, fifteen
4. 20, twenty
5. 25, twenty-five
6. 30, thirty
7. 35, thirty-five
8. 40, forty
9. 45, forty-five

PAGE 140

1. 10, ten
2. 20, twenty
3. 30, thirty
4. 40, forty
5. 50, fifty
6. 60, sixty

PAGE 141

1. 1, one
2. 2, two
3. 3, three
4. 4, four
5. 5, five
6. 6, six
7. 7, seven
8. 8, eight
9. 9, nine
10. 10, ten

PAGE 144–145

1. 35 ft
2. 30 m

PAGE 146

1. 5, five
2. 7, seven
3. 10, ten

PAGE 147

 =

 =

 =

 =

PAGE 148

1. £15, fifteen pounds
2. £4, four pounds
3. £25, twenty-five pounds
4. £32, thirty-two pounds

1. 1 minute

2. 2 minutes

3. 3 minutes

1. seven, 7:00
2. nine, 9:00
3. ten, 10:00
4. eight, 8:00
5. twelve, 12:00

6. half past two, 2:30
7. half past eight, 8:30
8. half past seven, 7:30
9. half past twelve, 12:30
10. half past six, 6:30

11. half past eleven, 11:30
12. half past ten, 10:30
13. nine, 9:00
14. ten, 10:00
15. one, 1:00

3

1

2

2

1

3

3

1

2

MEET THE MRS WORDSMITH TEAM

Editor-in-Chief
Sofia Fenichell

Associate Creative Director
Lady San Pedro

Art Director
Craig Kellman

Writers

Tatiana Barnes

Mark Holland
Sawyer Eaton

Amelia Mehra

Researcher
Eleni Savva

Lexicographer
Ian Brookes

Designers

Suzanne Bullat
James Sales

Fabrice Gourdel
James Webb
Holly Jones

Caroline Henriksen
Jess Macadam

Producers
Eva Schumacher Payne
Leon Welters

Academic Advisors
Emma Madden
Prof. Susan Neuman

Project Managers
Senior Editor Helen Murray
Design Manager Sunita Gahir

Senior Production Editor Jennifer Murray
Senior Production Controller Louise Minihane
Publishing Director Mark Searle

DK Delhi
DTP Designers Satish Gaur and Rohit Rojal
Senior DTP Designer Pushpak Tyagi
Pre-production Manager Sunil Sharma
Managing Art Editor Romi Chakraborty

DK would like to thank Roohi Sehgal and Julia March
for editorial assistance.

First published in Great Britain in 2021 by
Dorling Kindersley Limited
A Penguin Random House Company
DK, One Embassy Gardens, 8 Viaduct Gardens,
London, SW11 7BW

The authorised representative in the EEA is
Dorling Kindersley Verlag GmbH. Arnulfstr. 124,
80636 Munich, Germany.

Variations of this content are available as
printable worksheets at mrswordsmith.com

10 9 8 7 6 5 4 3
005–325947–August/2021

A CIP catalogue record for this book
is available from the British Library.
ISBN 978-0-24152-711-5

Printed and bound in Malaysia

www.dk.com

mrswordsmith.com

For the curious

This book was made with
Forest Stewardship Council™
certified paper – one small
step in DK's commitment to
a sustainable future.

The building blocks of reading

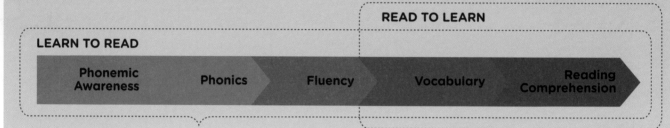

READ TO LEARN

LEARN TO READ

| Phonemic Awareness | Phonics | Fluency | Vocabulary | Reading Comprehension |

Readiculous App
App Store & Google Play

Word Tag App
App Store & Google Play

OUR JOB IS TO INCREASE YOUR CHILD'S READING AGE

This book adheres to the science of reading. Our research-backed learning helps children progress through phonemic awareness, phonics, fluency, vocabulary, and reading comprehension.